The Path
with Heart

The Path
with Heart

Michael Lynberg

Fawcett Columbine · New York

A Fawcett Columbine Book
Published by Ballantine Books

Library of Congress Catalog Card Number: 89-90915

ISBN: 0-449-90452-0

Cover design by Dale Fiorillo
Text design by Holly Johnson

Manufactured in the United States of America

First Edition: January 1990
10 9 8 7 6 5 4 3 2 1

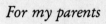

For my parents

I

The Meaning
of Success

What is the meaning of success?

For many of us, being successful means material and financial prosperity. How much money we make, the kind of car we drive, the quality of the house we live in—all of these are considered important measures of how we are doing in life. To a large degree, we judge each other and, ultimately, ourselves by what we have rather than by what we are or what we do.

But is success truly a matter of what we possess and of how much money we make? Does a well-furnished house make our lives worthwhile? Does an expensive automobile give us a sense of well-being and fulfillment?

Experience and common sense tell us that, while money and property are to a degree an important part of our lives, they do not necessarily make a person happy or at peace with himself. Our hearts and souls can starve in the midst of all the money and material possessions in the world; our greatest individual potential can lie dormant and unexplored, weighted down by visions of silver and gold. What is more, some of the most successful people who have ever lived are people who often had little or no money: Mahatma Gandhi died possessing only a pair of sandals, a robe, a staff, a spinning wheel, his spectacles, and a prayer book. Mozart was buried in an unmarked pauper's grave. Socrates cared more about a good conversation than about his next meal. Confucius was dependent on his small band of disciples. Rembrandt ended his life in austerity, as did Beethoven, Bach, and Van Gogh. Jesus died leaving only a robe for which the Roman soldiers cast lots.

None of these individuals was rich in a conventional sense. None of them had money or a large estate. Yet all of them, most would agree, lived great lives and were in their own way successful. Perhaps, then, success can mean more than just material and financial prosperity. Perhaps it is more than a matter of what we earn or possess.

Determining the meaning of success and the type of life we feel is most worth living is a difficult and personal affair. There are, to be sure, many ways to look at success, and perhaps no one definition is true to the exclusion of all others. Success can mean, among other things, contentment, health, good familial and social relations, and the realization of our unique talents and abilities. It can also mean integrity, faith, and the ability to enjoy life in all its variety and splendor.

Trying to define success takes us from the realm of science, with its impartial methods and precise formulations, into the world of philosophy, which is often more subjective and less conclusive. "The noblest of all studies," wrote Plato, "is the study of what man is and of what life he should live." This is philosophy's chief objective, and each individual who seeks the truth patiently, deliberately, and with an open mind, is in effect a philosopher. The answers we seek are often elusive, but we are almost always blessed for our efforts with greater understanding and tolerance; in a word, with greater wisdom.

During his trial, Socrates told the Athens court that the only reason he might be considered wiser than others was because he was profoundly aware of his own ignorance with regard to life's

The principal effect of the power of custom is to seize and ensnare us in such a way that it is hardly within our power to get ourselves back out of its grip and return unto ourselves to reflect and reason about its ordinances.

Montaigne

Thus to be independent of public opinion is the first formal condition of achieving anything great or rational whether in life or in science.

G.W.F. Hegel

We are prone to judge success by the index of our salaries or the size of our automobiles rather than by the quality of our service and relationship to humanity.

Martin Luther King, Jr.

most important matters. Life and our place in it are indeed perplexing. Trying to solve the problems of existence, even deciding how we can best live, is something like trying to solve a puzzle that has seemingly infinite variables, some of which can only be assumed. It is more than our limited faculties of reason and perception can handle. It is often easier to go along with what others say is right and to conform to standards and values which may not truly be our own.

At times this means measuring the quality and worth of our lives in dollars and cents. Our progress is commonly determined by our paycheck; our value by our investments. But many would agree that money and property may in fact have very little to do with our sense of happiness and fulfillment. "The impression forces itself upon one that men measure by false standards," contended Sigmund Freud, "that everyone seeks power, success, riches for himself and admires others who attain them while undervaluing the truly precious things in life." Perhaps the person whose life is dominated by the pursuit of wealth will become disillusioned and feel that he has been misguided, that the star by which he has navigated his life has led nowhere and left him stranded on a sea of discontent. Perhaps he will die with the highest and most precious part of his nature largely undeveloped and unexpressed. It is therefore vital that each of us examine the values by which he lives, to decide what is truly important and what will ultimately give him feelings of fulfillment and well-being. Socrates' maxim that the unexamined life is not worth living may be extreme, but at the very least the unexamined life is in danger of being misdirected and even wasted.

Through the years philosophers and writers have tried to define what in ethics is called "the good life"; that is, the way in which we can best make use of our brief worldly existence. For Socrates, self-knowledge is the chief good. For Aristotle, it is realizing our full potential as rational beings. For the Stoics like Epictetus and Seneca, the good life is one of discipline, self-denial and the development of character. It is ironic and sad that today the good life is largely identified as a life of ease and comfort, a life of wealth and plenty. The philosophers mentioned above, along with many others, would be highly critical of our present values. Two perspectives, however, with which contemporary man may feel more at home, define pleasure and power as the greatest goods to which we can aspire, goods which seem to correspond to our quest for money and material wealth.

Cyrenaic Hedonism, founded by Aristippus,

takes immediate pleasure to be the highest good in life. Man is by nature a pleasure seeking animal, and each opportunity for pleasure must be enjoyed in the full lest the opportunity be gone forever. "Eat, drink, and be merry, for tomorrow we may die," is the ethic practiced by the hedonists, and indeed, it is an ethic adhered to by many today as well (although we will often forego an immediate pleasure for one which we feel will be greater in the future). Having fun, retiring in luxury at an early age, grasping for all we can get—these goals are commonplace enough. Success in our society is largely determined by what a person can take or get, by how pleasant and comfortable he can make his life.

This propensity towards pleasure is not hard to understand. Not only is it in our nature to seek pleasure and avoid pain, but people today are often plagued by a sense of vagueness and futility, a feeling of emptiness which they try to fill. Science has made us increasingly aware of the smallness of our position in the cosmos. Our little planet circles a star which is one of billions of stars in a galaxy which is just one of billions of galaxies in a universe which itself is destined to decay and die. The history of our species (not to mention our own life spans) is but a blink in eternity. It seems that nothing we do, individually or collectively, can make much dif-

He who wishes to secure the good of others has
already secured his own.

Confucius

How far that little candle throws his beams!
So shines a good deed in a naughty world.

William Shakespeare

There is only one solution if old age is not to be
an absurd parody of our former life, and that is
to go on pursuing ends that give our existence a
meaning—devotion to individuals, to groups or
to causes, social, political, intellectual, or
creative work. . . . One's life has value so long as
one attributes value to the life of others, by
means of friendship, indignation, compassion.

Simone de Beauvoir

ference anyway. Compounding our sense of futility is the threat of nuclear annihilation, the knowledge that life as we know it could be wiped out because of some absurd dispute or misunderstanding. Or perhaps our promising species could fall prey to a mindless and incompassionate strand of RNA, a virus several thousand times smaller that the head of a pin, but highly contagious and capable of ending our lives without the slightest remorse. Given this pessimistic outlook and the insecurity it breeds, it is not surprising that so many in contemporary society make pleasure their purpose, giving their desires free reign, and taking as much as they can get while they can get it.

A second ethical philosophy by which contemporary man consciously or unconsciously lives defines power as the greatest good to which we can aspire. This point of view, foreseen but not advocated by Plato in the classics, has as its most articulate and passionate spokesman Friedrich Nietzsche. Living amidst the exciting changes in perspective brought on by Darwinism, Nietzsche saw the *will to power* as the underlying motive behind man's actions and the uninhibited realization of the will to power as the greatest good to which he can aspire. The history of evolution by natural selection is the history of one species triumphing over another for scarce resources, or of an individual within that species triumphing over its neighbor. To be strong is to survive, to be weak is to perish. Morality begins as a set of arbitrary rules invented by the weak "herd" to protect itself from strong individuals. Religion is morality taken to an extreme, with God's will and the threat of eternal punishment as its mandate. Nietzsche despised religion, especially Judaism and Christianity, because it teaches compassion and thereby preserves what is weak in our species, inhibiting what he believed to be the natural advancement of mankind.

Nietzsche's perspective is perhaps shocking, but the sentiment that man is by nature a selfish creature interested foremost in his own survival and well-being is commonplace, as is the sentiment that competition fosters progress and is ultimately for the good of the human race. Indeed, our free enterprise economy is predicated on competition, with weak businesses falling prey to stronger businesses, and weak individuals (as well as those who will not or cannot conform) sometimes sinking into poverty and surviving only because a rather thin and tattered social welfare net keeps them from falling into the abyss. Andrew Carnegie, a pioneer of industrial capitalism and one of the richest men in America at the turn of the century, wrote that the law of com-

Great deeds cannot die
They with the sun and moon renew their light
Forever, blessing those that look on them.
Alfred Lord Tennyson

No energy is lost in the world, nor is it merely
the souls of men that are immortal but all their
actions as well. They live on through their
effects.
Johann Wolfgang von Goethe

Let us endeavor to so live that when we come
to die even the undertaker will be sorry.
Mark Twain

What an extraordinary situation is that of us mortals! Each of us is here for a brief sojourn; for what purpose he knows not, though he sometimes thinks he feels it. But from the point of view of daily life, without going deeper, we exist for our fellow-men—in the first place for those on whose smiles and welfare all our happiness depends, and next for those unknown to us personally with whose destinies we are bound up by the tie of sympathy.

Albert Einstein

The tragedy of life is in what dies inside a man while he lives—the death of genuine feeling, the death of inspired response, the death of awareness that makes it possible to feel the pain or the glory of other men in oneself.

Norman Cousins

Loneliness and the feeling of being unwanted is the most terrible poverty.

Mother Teresa

petition cannot be avoided: "no substitutes have been found; and while the law may sometimes be hard on the individual, it is best for the race because it ensures the survival of the fittest in every department." John D. Rockefeller, also one of the wealthiest men of his time, said: "The growth of a large business is merely the survival of the fittest. . . . The American Beauty rose can be produced in the splendor and fragrance which bring cheer to its beholder only by sacrificing the early buds which grow up around it." Freedom of competition, it is therefore believed, is to be safeguarded; the will to power, the will to succeed, to be encouraged. In a sense, success today is a contest of power, the survival of the strongest and most able.

But do power and pleasure truly make us feel successful, or is there still something missing in our lives? Relative to much of the world, the majority of people in the United States and other Western democracies already live lives of plenty and have a great deal of power. There is, to be sure, a dreadful amount of poverty and want, but most of us are fortunate enough to have good food to eat, warm beds to sleep in, clothes to wear. Music, entertainment and other pleasures are bountiful. In comparison with the richest king of medieval times, even of a hundred years ago, many of us have remarkable es and opportunities. TV, radio, and telephones are things that we take for granted. Cashing our paycheck and walking into the nearest supermarket or department store is like having the goods of thousands of specialized servants at our disposal. Buses, subways, and cars can take us places faster than a team of twenty horses. We can even fly. Medical science and hygienic improvements have practically doubled our life expectancy and the survival rate of our children. But still, as relatively rich and powerful as we are, we want more. Many of us do not feel successful and we struggle to understand the sense of emptiness and alienation that sometimes permeates our lives.

What is the cause of our discontent? What can we do that will make us feel that our lives are more meaningful and worthwhile? The answer has been given by the great writers, thinkers, and spiritual leaders of each generation, but it seems to get continually lost in the constant shuffle and petty exigencies of daily life. At times, in our strident efforts to keep abreast of the fast pace and competitive nature of our modern world, we lose sight of what is truly important. We forget that true success is multifaceted, involving our complete, all-around development as human beings. It is not only a question of what we can take or receive, but also of what we give. It is growth, integrity, friendship, faith and love, and these do not so much come from what we possess, but from the pursuit of a worthy purpose, from making ourselves a worthwhile part of the world in which we live.

Albert Schweitzer, who spent fifty years of his life serving his fellow man in the oppressive heat of the African jungle, providing medical aid to those most desperately in need, said, "I don't know what your destiny will be, but one thing I do know: the only ones among you who will be really happy are those who have sought and found how to serve."

Leo Tolstoy wrote, "Life is a place of service, and in that service one has to suffer a great deal that is hard to bear, but more often to experience a great deal of joy. But that joy can be real only if people look upon their life as a service, and have a definite object outside themselves and their personal happiness."

Martin Luther King, Jr. observed, "Every man must decide whether he will walk in the light of creative altruism or in the darkness of destructive selfishness. This is the judgment. Life's most urgent question is, what are you doing for others?"

And Albert Einstein, in an article trying to define success, wrote, "Only a life lived for others is a life worthwhile."

The importance of giving, the path to a greater sense of success and fulfillment, is also a central lesson of the world's great religions. "They who give have all things," says a Hindu proverb, "they who withhold have nothing." In the Buddhist scriptures it is written, "The man of wisdom who did good, the man of morals who gave gifts, in this world and the next one too, they will advance to happiness." In the Koran, Mohammed conveys that "a man's true wealth is the good he does in this world." In the Torah, it is said that the Lord gives to "every man according to his ways, according to the fruit of his doings." And in Christianity we learn that "it is more blessed to give than to receive," and that "he who is greatest among you shall be your servant."

Indeed, none of us has a chance of living a great life, of continually fulfilling his highest needs and potentialities, except those who have looked for and found a way to serve. The great people of history, those who have earned our respect and admiration, those whom we can truly call successful, are people who have in some way enriched the lives of their fellow man. Whether it is Beethoven, Shakespeare, Renoir or Einstein, what is remembered and cherished is not how much money they made or how large a house they lived in, but how they help

Consciously or unconsciously, every one of us does render some service or other. If we cultivate the habit of doing this service deliberately, our desire for service will steadily grow stronger, and will make not only for our own happiness, but for that of the world at large.

Mahatma Gandhi

The interior joy we feel when we have done a good deed, when we feel we have been needed somewhere and have lent a helping hand, is the nourishment the soul requires. Without those times when man feels himself to be part of the spiritual world by his actions, his soul decays.

Albert Schweitzer

We are challenged on every hand to work
untiringly to achieve excellence in our lifework.
Not all men are called to specialized or
professional jobs; even fewer rise to the heights
of genius in the arts and sciences; many are
called to be laborers in factories, fields, and
streets. But no work is insignificant. All labor
that uplifts humanity has dignity and
importance and should be undertaken with
painstaking excellence. If a man is called to be a
street sweeper, he should sweep streets even as
Michelangelo painted, or Beethovewn composed
music, or Shakespeare wrote poetry. He should
sweep streets so well that all the host of heaven
and earth will pause to say, "Here lived a great
street sweeper who did his job well."

Martin Luther King, Jr.

What we do is nothing but a drop in the ocean;
but if we didn't do it, the ocean would be one
drop less.   *Mother Teresa*

us enjoy and understand our world; what is
brated is not the power that they held, but how
expressing what was highest and most noble in their
natures, they help us experience what is most ex-
alted in our own.

One does not have to compose a symphony
to live a great life; nor does one have to paint a
masterpiece or write a classic book. Each of us,
where we are, can make his work a gift to the world.
A parent raising children, a teacher inspiring stu-
dents, a business man or woman providing excellent
service—no matter where we are, we can do something to add to the quality of life of those around
us. The opportunity to do so is right before you, in
the thing you are about to do.

In making our work a gift to the world, in
making it an expression of our love for life, for God,
and for our fellow man, we fulfill our highest potential, our most beautiful destiny as human beings.
Why then do so many of us get sidetracked into
"lives of quiet desperation"? Why do so many of us
turn from the path with heart and travel the
crowded turnpikes of conformity and egoism?

II

Much Ado
About Money

The answer,
as we
have seen,

lies at least in part in our pursuit of what William James, in a letter to H.G. Wells, called "the bitch-goddess success;" that is, our society's "squalid cash interpretation" of the word success which, he said, "is our national disease." But is money really so bad? Is it truly the root of all evil? Is it to blame if our lives are not as fulfilling and meaningful as they might be?

Not money but the love of money, the pursuit of money to the exclusion of other worthy aims, is the root of our malady. Money is itself benign; it is merely a medium of exchange by which we trade the fruits of our labor for the products and services of others. As such, it is necessary for our very survival. With money, we indirectly exchange the goods we produce for food, shelter, and clothing; it pays for books, tuition and medical bills; in some cases, it can even help save lives.

"If money go before, all ways do lie open," says Shakespeare. Indeed, money can act like a lubricant that helps us move through life with greater ease and comfort, with less friction. It enables us to rest when we are tired or weary, it can give us the time and resources to cultivate our minds and our talents. Lack of money, on the other hand, can make our lives painfully cumbersome and difficult. Our options and our sense of freedom become limited; sometimes we have to take a job that we don't particularly like or acquiesce to terms that others dictate just in order to survive ("My poverty, but not my will, consents," again quoth Shakespeare). Moreover, when we are constantly preoccupied with our next meal or with a stack of unpaid bills, it becomes difficult, if not impossible, to pursue our higher aspirations and more worthy goals.

Money, therefore, is in itself not the great evil; it is, in fact, a necessary part of our relatively complicated lives should we choose to be a part of contemporary civilization. But if we make money our life's purpose, our raison d'être, we may be ruining our chances for a greater sense of success and well-being. "Money is a good servant," said Bacon, "but a bad master." The path we should take is thus a matter of personal reflection and judgment. The question of money, like so many other issues in philosophy and life, does not resolve itself neatly into black and white, right and wrong. It is incumbent on each of us to examine his life and the values by which he lives and to come up with his own sensible and moderate approach to money: what Aristotle would call the Golden Mean and what in Confucianism is called the Doctrine of the Mean. This will not be easy, however. Our best reason and judgment will always be counterbalanced by another part of our nature which can lead us astray, a part of ourselves which never seems satisfied with what we have and which always wants more.

There is an old Russian folktale, splendidly recounted by Tolstoy, about a peasant whose chief goal in life is to own more and more land. He already owns a farm of considerable size, but it is not enough and he wants more. When he hears that the government is practically giving away as much land as a man can claim in another part of the country, to promote that region's growth, the peasant takes temporary leave of his family and makes the long journey to seek his fortune.

Most of the luxuries and many of the so-called comforts of life are not only not indispensable, but positive hindrances to the elevation of mankind.   *Henry David Thoreau*

It is preoccupation with possession, more than anything else, that prevents us from living freely and nobly.   *Bertrand Russell*

He is a wise man who does not grieve for the things which he has not, but rejoices for those which he has.   *Epictetus*

The more a man lays stress on false possessions, and the less sensitivity he has for what is essential, the less satisfying is his life.   *Carl Jung*

Wealth is the parent of luxury and indolence, and poverty of meanness and viciousness, and both of discontent.   *Plato*

When he gets there he learns the rules of the transaction: he must begin at a specified point at sunrise and run or walk as far and as wide as he can by sunset. All of the land within the boarders he traverses will be his so long as he gets back before sundown. If he fails to get back on time, he gets no land and he does not get another chance to stake a claim.

The peasant is thrilled at the opportunity. He rests that night the best he can, and the next morning, as the first sliver of the sun peeks over the horizon, he sets out at a steady pace so as to conserve his energy. He starts by walking briskly north so that he can watch the ascent of the sun to his right. After going a very long way in this direction, he thinks that it would be prudent to turn east. But the land is so rich and so fertile that he simply must have more, so he goes just a little bit further to broaden his claim.

Finally, he drives a stake into the ground, turns east, and starts off in that direction. The sun is blazing hot now and he is covered with perspiration. His legs are heavy, but his ambition carries him forward. No longer able to see the place where he started, he again thinks it would be wise to turn and start in the next direction, but the land is too beautiful, he must own it, so he goes just a little bit further before driving another stake.

When he does turn south, his mouth is parched and his lungs ache. He feels that he cannot go on, but something inside pushes him forward. After today he will have plenty of time to rest.

The sun is descending as he turns west, on the last leg of his journey. The place where he started is still just a speck on the horizon; it will be a race for him to get back before the deadline. He lumbers forward, barely able to lift his legs. At last he can make out the place where he started and the faces of the people there. They are laughing at him.

The sun sinks heavy and orange; just a few minutes more. The tired peasant struggles to the finish line and falls over just as the last rays of the sun disappear over the horizon. He's made it. The land is his. But his victory is short-lived, for on the spot he collapses of exhaustion and dies.

What a tragic parable this is for our times. People everywhere are in a race for more land, more money, a bigger house, a better car. In many cases they run themselves into the grave, never stopping to enjoy the simple pleasures in life and to appreciate the many comforts that they already have. To paraphrase the proverb, many people spend their

To be without some of the things you want is an indispensable part of happiness.

Bertrand Russell

None of those who have been raised to a loftier height by riches and honors is really great. Why then does he seem great to you? It is because you are measuring the pedestal with the man.

Seneca

Beware of ambition for wealth; for there is nothing so characteristic of narrowness and littleness of soul as the love of riches; and there is nothing more honorable and noble than indifference to money.

Cicero

Are you not ashamed of heaping up the greatest
amount money and honor and reputation, and
caring so little about wisdom and truth and the
greates improvement of the soul, which you
never regard or heed at all?

Socrates

If a man owns land, the land owns him.
Ralph Waldo Emerson

Possessions, outward success, publicity, luxury—
to me these things have always been
contemptible. I believe that a simple and
unassuming manner of life is best for everyone,
best for both the body and the mind.
Albert Einstein

health acquiring wealth, and then spend their wealth trying to regain their health.

What is it in man that causes him to desire money and property and then, when he has them, to want more? Or as Thoreau asked, "Why should we be in such desperate haste to succeed and in such desperate enterprises?"

There is doubtless something in our genetic makeup that accounts for our acquisitiveness, our desire for property and material possessions. Many other forms of life also have a tendency to build a nest or home, to protect it tenaciously, to stock it with provisions, and then to add to its store. Squirrels stow away nuts and berries; the family dog hides a bone; an ant struggles with a prize twig or morsel of food several times its own size, lifting, pushing, and dragging it back to what one hopes is a hero's welcome on the hill; a bumblebee diligently passes from one flower to the next, collecting more and more pollen before finally retiring to the hive. In all of nature (even down to the cellular and microcellular level), those survive who are able to fend for themselves and their families, protecting their territory and securing food and other necessities. Perhaps this explains, at least in part, the human compulsion for property and possessions: like our friends the ant and the bumblebee, there could be something deep in our nature that compels us to build a home, to seek provisions, and then, when we have them, to go out and seek more (sometimes we even try to carry more than we can comfortably afford). Our ancestors who did not have these instincts simply did not survive and reproduce in a less civilized world.

Much of human behavior, however, is learned, and to this biological impetus we can presently add others which are cultural in nature. To begin with, we in America are heirs to a legacy of frontierism. Our ancestors who came to this land from all parts of the world often left severe repression and austerity (an exception is our black ancestors who were cruelly brought here against their will). They came in search of opportunity and fortune; often they were willing to endure significant hardships in order to build a better life for themselves and their families.

Once here, the new Americans built great cities and rapidly pushed from east to west, always seeking a new frontier, a new opportunity for wealth and prosperity. Along the way, they were sometimes blinded by their ambition, committing terrible atrocities: the blacks from Africa were enslaved, bought and sold like animals, and forced to build the fortunes of their white captors; an entire race of native Americans was virtually exterminated and the land soaked with innocent blood; with the advent of the Industrial Revolution, the nation's air, water and precious natural resources began to be mindlessly exploited and sometimes irreparably damaged. Nevertheless, what people found fascinating were the stories of those who made it, of those who struck it rich, thus feeding the fire of frontierism.

Today, this spirit of frontierism endures; in a figurative sense, Americans are still pushing west, riding toward the proverbial sunset of more land, more money, more and better material possessions. We are still fascinated with stories of those who succeed (especially if their success is fast and easy), for, if they made it, then surely we can, too. However, when we do not find success forthcoming, when the soil we till does not yield a quick harvest, many of us become frustrated and anxious. We look for a new frontier, but today's opportunities seem increasingly specialized and technical—they may take years of hard work and preparation. Sometimes an individual (or a group of individuals) feels that there is no way left for him to make it, that the American promise of abundance has been broken, that the dream is a lie. Sometimes he quiets his ambition and native restlessness in drink or drugs; sometimes the tension is released in the form of crime and antiso-

Better is a little with righteousness
Than great revenue with injustice.

Proverbs 16:8

For the love of money is the root of all evil:
which while some coveted after, they have erred
from the faith, and pierced themselves through
with many sorrows.   *I Timothy 6:10*

He that maketh haste to be rich shall not be
innocent.   *Proverbs 28:20*

Riches are not from an abundance of worldly
goods, but from a contented mind.   *The Koran*

Man is born with his hands clenched, but his
hands are open in death, because on entering the
world he desires to grasp everything, but on
leaving, he takes nothing away.   *The Talmud*

cial behavior—he strikes back at those who have teased and misled him; he breaks the rules for which he feels contempt.

The tension many feel, the painful hunger for material and financial success, is heightened by the way in which our economy works. "The truth is," said Woodrow Wilson, "we are caught in a great economic system which is heartless," and at times he may be right. Although we are blessed with remarkable freedom, sometimes this freedom is abused for personal gain. Our free enterprise system thrives on consumerism, on the constant exchange of goods and currency. If the public does not buy a certain product, then the company (or division) that produces that product will soon go out of business, and the people employed by the company may find themselves out of work. It is therefore necessary that the company create the need for its product, and this need, while sometimes real, can often be based on a whole variety of human emotions and weaknesses. A new car may appeal to our desire to look prosperous, a cosmetic product to our fear of getting old in a society that promotes and worships youth (Carl Jung said that only they fear getting old who are not living their lives fully in the present). The marketplace is therefore crowded with all manner of products and luxuries that are, to quote

Thoreau, "not only not indispensable, but positive hindrances to the elevation of mankind." We think that we need the latest in fashion, cars and appliances because we are persuaded, through clever advertising and promotion, to think this way. In reality, we may be just as happy, if not happier, without them, or at least with something more simple. Certainly, we would have more freedom to pursue our higher ideals if we were not spending our precious time and energy earning enough money to follow the latest trend.

So alluring is this treadmill of consumerism, however, that we almost entirely judge our success and that of others by what we have or what we can buy. Money and possessions are something tangible by which we have come to measure the progress and value of our lives; a way of keeping score, if you will, a way of assessing our worth. Very few of us, unfortunately, have the courage and self-knowledge to do without such external rewards and to follow our own cherished vision, our own standard of success. Vincent van Gogh sold only one painting in his entire career and was dependent on the generous but limited support of his brother. Still, he went on working and pursuing excellence; sometimes he would not eat for days so that he could afford to buy more materials with which to paint. Walt Whitman sent his self-published book of poems, *Leaves of Grass*, to writers and literary critics across the country, hoping it would find acceptance. Instead, it was met with almost universal ridicule and rejection. His only solace was a note from Ralph Waldo Emerson, who encouraged him to keep writing, which of course he did. Johann Sebastian Bach was also panned by the critics of his day. The only decent commission he ever received was to compose a relaxing set of pieces for the clavichord, the Goldberg Variations, for a Russian envoy who had trouble falling asleep. Beyond this, he generally struggled to provide for his large family (eleven of his twenty children died in childhood) by playing the organ at church services. Michelangelo lived a modest and solitary life ("Painting is my wife," he said; "my works are my children.") with few luxuries and comforts. Characteristically, he was willing to refuse compensation, some biographers claim, for his work on the Sistine Chapel, a staggering project which took him years to complete, because he feared that money would corrupt the integrity of his vision.

Such courage is as rare as genius. Many of us do not have a strong enough sense of purpose or identity to forego external rewards and to pursue our own idea of success. We put off developing our

Too many people spend money they haven't earned, to buy things they don't want, to impress people they don't like.   *Will Rogers*

The fashion wears out more apparel than the man.   *William Shakespeare*

Remember this, that very little is needed to make a happy life.   *Marcus Aurelius*

That which makes poverty a burden, makes riches also a burden. It matters little whether you lay a sick man on a wooden or a golden bed, for whithersoever he be moved he will carry his malady with him.   *Seneca*

Money may be the husk of many things, but not the kernel. It brings you food, but not appetite; medicine, but not health; acquaintances, but not friends; servants, but not faithfulness; days of joy, but not peace or happiness.   *Henrik Ibsen*

most cherished talents and push aside our youthful dreams to pursue something which seems more tangible and secure. Consequently, a part of our being remains unfulfilled. Only later in life, when we see that money and property cannot fill our sense of emptiness, do we realize the magnitude of our mistake. Hopefully then we will attempt to truly live the precious days that remain by, as Simone de Beauvoir said, "pursuing ends that give our existence a meaning."

We may also let the pursuit of material and financial prosperity take precedence over our relations with friends and loved ones. Perhaps we are not in love or have not been able to form lasting and meaningful relationships; or maybe we are married and having difficulties with our spouse or children. For a while, the pursuit of money and possessions can help keep our minds off these problems by becoming the object of our attention and affection. Moreover, our money and possessions will not leave us for somebody else; they won't talk back or disappoint us; they are something we can hold on to and control. Often too late, when, in our ambition for riches, we have already alienated both family and friends, when we have already denied ourselves the chance to feel and express love, do we realize that we are missing out on life's greatest adventure. For it is above all with those to whom we are close that we have an opportunity to give and to share, thus fulfilling our highest potential, thus realizing our most profound joy.

Perhaps the most compelling reason behind our pursuit of riches is that we are trying to make up for the feelings of insecurity and the lack of self-esteem that are so tragically prevalent in our culture. From birth to death we are sold on an image of the good life that, as we have seen, is at least in part promulgated by companies trying to get us to buy their products and services. We grow up taking for granted that success means a certain lifestyle, certain mandatory possessions, a certain image of beauty and youth. If we don't hold to this image, or if we cannot afford the proper amenities, then we are led to believe that something is missing in our lives, that we are in some way deficient. The terrible thing is that many of us believe it. We go through life feeling unworthy, unattractive, not allowing others to love or respect us, denying ourselves the happiness and depth of experience that we so richly deserve, because we fall short of some arbitrary image or ideal. The truth is, we will always fall short. No matter how much money we have or how many elegant possessions clutter our lives, we can always have more, we can always want

something newer and better (and there will al
be somebody there trying to sell it to us). No matter
how much power we wield, there will always be
another vista to conquer. No matter how beautiful
we can make ourselves look, we still must grow old
and die. Take a moment to consider: if you are not
happy or at peace with what you possess in life right
now, then you may never be. The reason is simple:
happiness and peace of mind come mostly from
contentment with who you are, what you do, what
direction your life is taking, not with what you have
or possess.

What is also dangerous in our society is that
if the success and riches which we so desperately
need to feel good about ourselves are not immedi-
ately forthcoming, if the seeds we sow do not
quickly grow to fruition, then we can at least create
the *appearance* of success. We can borrow money to
buy the house or the car that we need; we can take
out credit to purchase the right clothes and acces-
sories. Americans are generally an impatient and
restless people; especially in this age of push button
technology, we are used to things being fast and
easy. Credit enables us to have what we want *right
now*, without the pain of having to work and wait
for what could be months or years. We are also an
optimistic people, and this natural optimism can be

A man in debt is so far a slave.
Ralph Waldo Emerson

Neither a borrower nor a lender be,
For loan oft loses both itself and friend,
And borrowing dulls the edge of husbandry.
William Shakespeare

He is rich enough who owes nothing.
French Proverb

He that goes a-borrowing goes a-sorrowing.
English Proverb

The borrower is the servant of the lender.
Proverbs 20:7

both our strength and our downfall. We expect the best for ourselves, and rightly so. Often we will get the raise that we anticipate; often our investments will pay off. But, after we have borrowed against these anticipated earnings, we sometimes find that our golden tomorrow brings its own needs and desires. The car for which we took out a loan is now having engine problems; the clothes we bought on credit are now worn and out of style. Thus in many cases we go on borrowing and buying, trying to quench our unending thirst for more and better, lugging behind us a load of debts.

These debts can have a paralyzing effect on our independence to pursue our higher ideals, on our ability to live successful and fulfilling lives. Credit can presently give us greater freedom and opportunity, but down the line we may pay for this freedom and opportunity with compounded interest. It may no longer be possible for us to change careers or to take a risk and pursue our life's dream because we need the money we are earning just to cover our bills. It may no longer be possible for us to take a leave of absence to be with our family or to travel and see part of the world's rich tapestry of cultures because we need to keep working just to pay for what we have already used up, eaten, and worn out.

Credit, of course, is not all bad; like money, it has its good side and it seems to be an integral part of our complicated lives in contemporary society. Credit can enable us to invest in the home of our dreams, the place where we feel we can create the best environment to raise our family; it can enable us to start a business and to bring a valuable product or service to the marketplace; it can help us take advantage of an opportunity which we feel may never occur again; it can get us through a difficult time or an emergency to which we might otherwise succumb. Like money, credit can be both a blessing and a curse. It is largely a question of our judgment in using it.

How then can we employ better judgment with regard to money and credit so that we may be able to live greater and more fulfilling lives? The key, put simply, is to diminish our wants. Man's basic needs for food, shelter, and clothing are relatively simple and easy to procure, but, as Epicurus wrote, "the wealth of vain fancies recedes to infinity." No matter how hard we try, no matter how much we struggle, we will always be one step behind our desire for more. Our freedom and contentment, therefore, lie in curbing our unlimited wants, rather than in trying to fulfill them, which is impossible. "It is not the man who has little, but the man who craves more, that is poor," says Seneca. "A man is rich in proportion to the number of things which he can afford to let alone," writes Thoreau. "He will always be a slave who does not know how to live upon a little," states Horace.

Upon reflection, most of us already have everything that can be enjoyed by the richest person in the world: we can sleep in only one bed, under one roof, at a time; we can wear one set of clothes, drive one car, and eat one meal at a time. Having a mansion with dozens of rooms, closets full of clothes, and a driveway lined with cars is really superfluous. All these possessions may make us feel secure, but true security comes not from what we own (which can always be lost, stolen, or worn-out), but from confidence in who we are and in what we can do; they may win us the respect and admiration of others, but such respect is often shallow and opportunistic, and such admiration is sometimes nothing more than smiling envy. Moreover, filling our lives with property and possessions can actually take away our freedom to fulfill our higher needs. When we own something—a house, a car, whatever—it also owns a piece of us, proportionate to the importance we assign it in our lives. If we value property, then that property takes up a space in our heart, acting like a sponge and soaking up

We should aim rather at leveling down our
desires than leveling up our means.

Aristotle

Can anything be so elegant as to have few
wants, and to serve them one's self?

Ralph Waldo Emerson

One is not rich by what one owns, but more by
what one is able to do without with dignity.

Immanuel Kant

Civilization, in the real sense of the term,
consists not in the multiplication but in the
deliberate and voluntary restriction of wants.
This alone promotes happiness and contentment,
and increases the capacity for service.

Mahatma Gandhi

He who is taught to live upon little owes more
to his father's wisdom than he who has a great
deal left him does to his father's care.

William Penn

the love and passion that we could be channeling towards growth and more creative pursuits. "The ransom of a man's life," says the Old Testament, "are his riches."

It is therefore imperative that we keep our wants within reason, curbing our natural propensity to hoard and collect, so that we can be freer to develop our talents and to give. We purchase our material possessions with money, but we purchase our money with our time and energy, in a word, with our lives. Indirectly, therefore, you are purchasing the property and material possessions which you so highly value with your life. It is up to you to decide whether you are paying too much or whether the transaction is just.

III

Your Gift
to the World

"I have not the shadow of a doubt,"

said Mahatma Gandhi, "that any man or woman can achieve what I have if he or she would make the same effort and cultivate the same hope and faith. . . . I know that I have still before me a difficult path to traverse."

At first glance, Gandhi's statement may seem a bit too optimistic. Very few are those who actually succeed in matching the strength, discipline, and self-sacrifice of the physically unimposing man from India, the man who, more than anyone else at the time, shaped the events of one of the world's largest nations, insisting on the freedom and dignity of his people, willing to suffer (he spent a great deal of his life in prison) and even die (he fasted a total of sixteen times, sometimes to the threshold of death) in order to affect change and win victory for his fellow man. As Einstein eulogized after Gandhi's tragic death, "Generations to come, it may be, will scarce believe that such a one as this ever in flesh and blood walked upon this earth."

Nonetheless, Gandhi's proclamation is correct in that each of us, even though we may often fall short, at least has the potential to live great and fulfilling lives. It is largely a question of the effort we make, of the intensity of our desire to pay back at least part of the debt we owe to God and to Life for the miracle of our existence.

The path we must traverse, however, is indeed a difficult one. We are marvelously complex creatures with many conflicting desires and impulses. In part, we are the result of billions of years of genetic evolution in which one individual or species has survived and prospered often at the expense of another (even by eating that other), in a cruel and intricate contest of strength and adaptability. At the same time, we humans are gifted with this remarkable, godlike consciousness of ourselves and of the process that, with our unique capacity for reason, makes us realize that cooperation

We cannot live only for ourselves. A thousand
fibers connect us with our fellow-men; and
along those fibers, as sympathetic threads, our
actions run as causes, and they come back to us
as effects.

Herman Melville

No man is an Island intire of it self; every man
is a peece of the Continent, a part of the maine;
if a clod be washed away by the sea, Europe is
the lesse . . . Any man's death diminishes me
because I am involved in Mankinde.

John Donne

We are members one of another.

Ephesians 4:25

We can be thankful to a friend for a few acres, or for a little money; yet for the freedom and command of the whole earth and for the great benefits of our being, our life, health, and reason, we look at ourselves as under no obligation.

Seneca

Many times a day I realize how much my own outer and inner life is built upon the labors of my fellow men, both living and dead, and how earnestly I must exert myself in order to give in return as much as I have received.

Albert Einstein

The future of humanity depends upon each person striving, in whatever situation he finds himself, to manifest true humanity to men.

Albert Schweitzer

can be man's greatest strength, and compassion his greatest salvation. Thus have arisen culture and civilization.

Each of us has the power, to a significant degree, to shape the course of his or her life and destiny. We can yield to our selfish and greedy impulses, which seem to come so naturally and which do not require nearly so much discipline or self-control, or we can walk a different path, following the dictates of our conscience, making our lives a service to our fellow man, and thereby fulfilling that part of ourselves which is highest, most noble, and most uniquely human. Like a composer, we can, with passion tempered by discipline, make beautiful music from the cacophony of our desires and impulses; like a master artist, we can paint a beautiful portrait from the colorful pallet of our motives and aspirations. How seriously we take this task will make our lives a masterpiece worthy of admiration and remembrance, or a botched and unfinished work worth little more than the materials used to produce it.

That our commitment and ability to serve affects the course of our lives has been a lesson of many of the world's great religions. "Give and it shall be given to you," said Jesus, "good measure, pressed down, and shaken together, and running over." In the Torah, it is written that "whatsoever a man soweth, that shall he also reap." In the Talmud, it is said that "according to the measure that one metes out to others, so is it meted out to him." In Buddhism and Hinduism, we encounter the complex doctrine of Karma, and how this world is a sort of spiritual school and testing ground where, in a procession of different lives, we are rewarded and punished for our actions and where, in serving God and our fellow man, we can evolve to a higher, more enlightened, and ultimately blissful state.

These religions are, of course, mostly concerned with our spiritual (and psychological) well-being. However, the idea that what we give in life determines what we receive has, by others, been given a more worldly and materialistic interpretation. Ralph Waldo Emerson states that, "If you love and serve men, you cannot, by any hiding or stratagem, escape remuneration." Elsewhere he says, "Life is a perpetual instruction in cause and effect.... The nature and soul of things takes on itself the guarantee of the fulfillment of every contract, so that honest service cannot come to a loss."

Emerson was, perhaps, influenced by the Newtonian perspective of a balanced and orderly world which prevailed in his day. Every action, said

Man is not born to solve the problem of the universe, but to find out what he has to do; and to restrain himself within the limits of his comprehension.

Johann Wolfgang von Goethe

Let him that would move the world move first himself.

Socrates

To have a great purpose to work for, a purpose larger than ourselves, is one of the secrets of making life significant; for then the meaning and worth of the individual overflow his personal borders, and survive his death.

Will Durant

The great use of life is to spend it for something that will outlast it.

William James

Insofar as man partakes of (the creative process) does he partake of the divine, of God, and that participation is his immortality. . . . His true destiny as cocreator in the universe is his dignity and his grandeur.

Alfred North Whitehead

You work that you may keep pace with the earth and the soul of the earth. For to be idle is to become a stranger unto the seasons, and to step out of life's procession, that marches in majesty and proud submission towards the infinite.

Kahlil Gibran

Newton, produces an equal and opposing reaction, every cause produces its commensurate effect. Newton, of course, derived this law from physical phenomena that could be observed, quantified, and understood. Emerson, however, took the idea of cause and effect one step further and applied it to human behavior and relations, where it also seemed to be valid. If you work hard and provide excellent and honest service, then you must sooner or later be compensated for this service. The value will be recognized and rewarded; the cause creates the effect. Conversely, if you are dishonest, if you cheat your fellow man or provide inferior service, then in time the truth will catch up and you will receive your fair and equal punishment. Such is the nature of things.

But is this true? Do we live in a just and orderly world where people always get what they deserve? It is comforting to think that we do; however, unless our rewards and punishment are carried out on a spiritual or psychological level which is difficult for us to understand or assess, experience seems to prove otherwise. All too often the seeds we sow and nurture to fruition get swept away by flood, eaten by locusts, or ravaged by drought. We may work very hard, produce superior results, be honest and sincere, yet the world does not beat a path to our door; circumstances beyond our control—perhaps a malevolent employer, an unreceptive public, or the vicissitudes of the marketplace—prevent us from getting back what we feel is materially (or even immaterially in terms of prestige or recognition) our just reward. Worse yet, any of us may fall victim to senseless tragedy and suffering—an act of nature, perhaps—that cuts our life short or otherwise prevents us from enjoying material success.

It therefore does not seem that we live in a perfectly just and orderly world, at least one that we are capable of understanding. Thus, while there is truth to what Emerson says about our actions and service shaping the material quality of our lives, this is not a position that can be defended too dogmatically. Interestingly, contemporary physicists have come to recognize something called the uncertainty principle, first put forth by Werner Heisenberg. In brief, it says that a given cause does not necessarily produce a consistent and predictable effect, that there is a significant variance in the empirical results that we get in observing certain phenomena, caused at least in part by the human measuring of these phenomena. At times something quite out of the ordinary can even happen, as if fundamental particles enjoyed a free will of their own. However, these

Although the world is full of suffering, it is also full of the overcoming of it.

Helen Keller

In scattering the seed, scattering your 'charity', your kind deeds, you are giving away in one form or another, part of your personality, and taking into yourself part of another. He who has received them from you will hand them to another. And how can you tell what part you may have in the future determination of the destinies of humanity?

Fyodor Dostoyevsky

The measure of a man's life is the well spending of it, and not the length.

Plutarch

Not one of us knows what effect his life produces, and what he gives to others; that is hidden from us and must remain so, though we are often allowed to see some little fraction of it, so that we may not lose courage.

Albert Schweitzer

The power of a man's virtue should not be measured by his special efforts, but by his ordinary doings.

Blaise Pascal

That best portion of a good man's life,
His little, nameless, unremembered acts,
Of kindness and of love.

William Wordsworth

varying results tend to average out, a pattern emerges, and we can make reasonable estimates of the outcome of certain experiments and phenomena. This uncertainty principle seems to be more true of our experiences in life as well. Our actions do not always produce commensurate effects. Sometimes we are rewarded materially for what we give, sometimes we are not. Sometimes something totally unpredictable and unfair happens. But over time, and up to our death (which seems a rather extreme effect suffered by us all), the ups and downs in life do tend to average out, a pattern emerges, and what we give can to a significant degree determine what we materially receive.

Much more important than what we receive, however, is that in giving, in serving our fellow man, we each make an impression upon the world, thereby contributing to the hope and destiny of mankind. "One of the signs of passing youth," wrote Virginia Woolf, "is the birth of a sense of fellowship with other human beings as we take our place among them." Indeed, our personal existence is intricately connected and intertwined with that of others; those of us who guard the flame of life today are children of the past, parents of the future. It is at once both thrilling and sobering to know that our actions and deeds, the way in which we choose to live, have an effect on those around us, and that these people in turn have an effect on others, and so on, in an endless chain of mutual influence and dependency. Each of us, in his own way, helps shape the world around him. Together we shape the future of mankind.

There is a parable in the Talmud in which a traveler comes upon an old man planting a carob tree. "When will the tree bear fruit?" asks the traveler. "Oh, perhaps in seventy years," replies the old man. "Do you expect to live to eat the fruit of that tree?" "No," says the old man, "but I didn't find the world desolate when I entered it, and as my fathers planted for me before I was born, so do I plant for those who come after me."

There is a valuable lesson in this parable: each of us who chooses to live has a responsibility to life. Not only are we indebted to those who have come before us for their good deeds and travail, but we are also each indebted for the gift of life, which we know is something precious and magnificent beyond our comprehension. The minutes and seconds of our existence are more precious than any fortune in currency or gold; each breath we draw more valuable than any parcel of land. It is through giving, through shaping the world around us in our own best image and acting with what Schweitzer called *reverence for life*, that we repay this debt and fulfill our greatest potential as human beings.

It has long been a problem in religion, and an argument for some against religious faith, that there cannot be an all-powerful and compassionate God who allows suffering. If He is compassionate and does not put and end to the pain in this world, then He must not be omnipotent. If He is omnipotent and does not eradicate suffering, then He must not be compassionate.

This, to be sure, is a difficult problem. But perhaps it is that God has given *us* the consciousness and ability to alleviate suffering. Perhaps, like a parent who gives his children every opportunity and encouragement to grow and become the best that they are capable of becoming, God has left it to us to fulfill our highest potential, expressing our love and compassion, and thereby shaping the destiny of the world. To be sure, we at almost every moment of our lives can do something to make this world the place we wish it to be, whether it is in providing food and relief for the hungry, fighting disease, protecting the earth's ecological system, helping a friend through a difficult time, or alleviating someone's loneliness with a kind word and friendly smile. This is what gives life meaning. This is the highest path we can follow.

If we live according to the guidance of reason,
we shall desire for others the good which we
seek for ourselves.

Baruch Spinoza

The highest wisdom is kindness.

The Talmud

Help thy brother's boat across and lo! thine
own has reached the shore.

Hindu Proverb

The whole world of loneliness, poverty, and
pain make a mockery of what human life
should be.

Bertrand Russell

The sole meaning of life is to serve humanity.

Leo Tolstoy

Once we become conscious of life and our place in it, once we become aware of our debt to God and to our fellow man, a part of us, that part which is highest and most uniquely human, can never be fulfilled if we turn our backs on our responsibility. Martin Luther King, Jr. once said, "As long as there is poverty in the world, I can never be rich, even if I have a billion dollars. As long as diseases are rampant and millions of people in this world cannot expect to live more than twenty-eight or thirty years, I can never be totally healthy, even if I just got a good checkup at the Mayo Clinic. I can never be what I ought to be until you are what you ought to be. This is the way the world is made. No individual or nation can stand out boasting of being independent. We are interdependent."

The hope and salvation of mankind lie in our becoming aware of our interdependence, of our responsibility to life and to our fellow man. Often we look outside of ourselves to a political system or idealogy as the solution to our problems. But no political idealogy can guarantee lasting change. The best that a political system can do—and this indeed is of great importance—is to educate its citizens ("Virtue is knowledge," said Socrates) and to give them the freedom, both in terms of expression and in terms of providing for their basic needs, so that

.dividuals who comprise that system can pur-
what is most noble in their natures, so that they
may follow the path with heart and make their lives
a service to their fellow man. "Which government
is best?" asked Goethe. "That which teaches us to
govern ourselves." A political system will only be
as ideal as its individual citizens. The only effective
change that can take place in this world is in the
hearts of men.

What is it that you can do to fulfill your
responsibility to life, to make your existence deeper,
more fulfilling and more meaningful? To begin with
you can make your work, whatever it is that you
do, a gift to the world. You don't have to be a
Gandhi, a Mozart, a Socrates, or an Einstein to make
a difference in the world, to live a significant life.
Whatever it is that you do, whether you are a parent, a doctor, a mechanic, a businessman, an artist,
or a politician, you can make your work an expression of your highest ideal, of your love and compassion for life and your fellow man.

But giving goes beyond our work. It is the
way we express ourselves, the way we relate to the
world around us. Much of the teaching and wisdom
of the world's great religions can be summed up in
the maxim to act towards others as we would like

them to act towards us. All the rest is commentary, says the Talmud. Indeed, it is in following this Golden Rule, in habitually expressing our love and kindness to those closest in our lives, in helping a stranger in need, in treating others the way that we ourselves would like to be treated, that we actually break free from the limits of our personal concerns and expand to the broader interests of life and of humanity. Giving is transcendental.

Sometimes we turn from this path with heart, giving only what is left over when our personal wants have been temporarily satisfied, reaching only for the spare change that lies in our pockets; sometimes we ignore the dictates of our conscience and rationalize that others, for whatever reason, are unworthy of receiving what we have to give. In so doing, we deprive ourselves of life's most fulfilling experience and we deprive the world of our unique and special gift. We forget that the borders that separate us are arbitrary, that underneath our age and the color of our skin, behind our faith in different religions and creeds, lie human beings who feel and suffer equally. Every human being deserves our love and respect, just as we merit the love and respect of others. As Gibran so elegantly wrote, "Surely he who is worthy to receive his days and

Judaism: What is hateful to you, do not to your fellow man. That is the entire law; all the rest is commentary. *The Talmud, Shabbat 31*

Christianity: As ye would that men should do to you, do ye also to them likewise. *Luke 6:31*

Buddhism: Hurt not others in ways that you yourself would find hurtful. *Udana Varga*

Hinduism: This is the sum of duty: Do naught unto others which would cause you pain if done to you. *The Mahabharata*

Taoism: Regard your neighbor's gain as your own gain, and your neighbor's loss as your own loss. *Tai Shang Kam Ying Rien*

Confucianism: "Is there one word that will keep us on the path to the end of our days?"
   "Yes, Reciprocity. What you do not wish yourself, do not unto others." *The Analects*

his nights, is worthy of all else from you who has deserved to drink from the ocean of deserves to fill his cup from your little stream."

Giving is, therefore, a way of being. As such it is the great imperative of our day. The issue of how we can best live and what we should do with our invaluable existence is more than just an intellectual game; it is even more than a question of how we can feel most happy and successful. It is now a matter of survival. We live in a perilous age; our remarkable species has, in its selfish quest for power and riches, brought the world to the brink of destruction. In so many ways we have fallen tragically short of our ideals, of what life could be. But we have also, at times, in our work and in our deeds, displayed our capacity for love, compassion and excellence. In this we hold the key to our survival and well-being. The choice is ours. You take part in this choice in the life you decide to live.